That Other Life

Books by Joyce Sutphen

Straight Out of View
Coming Back to the Body
Naming the Stars
Fourteen Sonnets
To Sing Along the Way (edited with Connie Wanek and Thom Tammaro)
First Words
House of Possibility
After Words
Modern Love & Other Myths
The Green House
Carrying Water to the Field
This Long Winter
That Other Life

That Other Life

Joyce Sutphen

Carnegie Mellon University Press
Pittsburgh 2023

Acknowledgments

I'm grateful to the editors of the following publications in which these poems, sometimes in different versions, first appeared:

Emprise Review: "After Reading a Postcard from Wallace Stevens"
The Gettysburg Review: "Marriage," "Losing Faith," and "The Hired Man"
Great River Review: "In New Jersey" and "Moses"
The New Republic: "The Red Kayak"
The Same: "Setting Type with Walt Whitman"
Split Rock Review: "Between the Stars"
Unearthed: "Reading Blake," "At Bowdoin," "Moving to the Mountains," and "How
    We Made It to California"
Water-Stone Review: "Forgotten Dreams"

"Berryman's Hands" appeared in *Berryman's Fate: A Centenary Celebration in Verse*,
edited by Philip Coleman. "Floater" appeared in *Nodin Poetry Anthology*, edited by
Monica DeGrazia and Emilio DeGrazia. "The Wordsworth Effect," "The Owl," and
"Reading Stanley Plumly" appeared in *The Writer's Almanac*.

I am grateful to Connie Wanek, Phil Dentinger, and Walter Cannon for the
friendship and inspiration that sustained me through the pandemic to *That Other
Life*. We began reading Shakespeare's plays together, first on Zoom, then in
backyards and on decks, and finally in person (so far fifteen). Sometimes we read
new poems to each other. Working with Connie Amoroso of Carnegie Mellon has
been a pleasure; her warm and careful attention to detail has made this a better
book. Special thanks to Walt for reading the manuscript in its many iterations. Of
course, errors that remain belong to me.

Cover image: *Central Park and the Plaza*, William A. Coffin, Smithsonian American
Art Museum, Bequest of Henry Ward Ranger through the National Academy of
Design

Book designed by Alayna Tillman

Library of Congress Control Number 2023933230
ISBN 978-0-88748-695-1

10 9 8 7 6 5 4 3 2 1

Contents

And Then

That

And At Last

This is for all the people, mostly nameless now, who were up in Russell's Gulch, out in the apple orchards, and down in Oakland. This is for all the kind souls along the way.

First

In a Brief Segment

We existed. We lived in places
with addresses that always changed.

We rearranged our rooms, we exchanged
rings (and other things).

For a short while we believed. We
witnessed a leaf and pronounced it green;

the air was blue when it turned to sky. Why
shouldn't the moon be cut in pieces?

Even to say it was brief is to say
too much, as much as I want

to claim more, and segment signals
a lingering longer than I meant.

For a moment, we existed, and afterwards
the world was always (briefly) ours.

527 5th Ave. S. E.

It was the perfect apartment—just beyond
positively 4th Street, and all of us
young and earnest in ways we've never stopped

being. It's where we first heard Neil Young's
Everybody Knows This Is Nowhere
and Dylan's *Nashville Skyline*. It's where we

sat together in the kitchen the day
our friends argued with their draft boards
and the night they did some damage in St. Paul.

We went back there after the convention
in Chicago, after all the protests
and Kent State, just before we were

scattering in the wind, just as The Band
pulled in . . . with regards for everyone.

Reading Blake in 1968

He put his long fingers (Ichabod Crane,
I thought to myself) together and looked

at us. It was 1968, early January,
and the radiators (well what?) were

clanking in the upper hell of Lind
(did it sing like a nightingale?) Hall.

Fingertips touching, tip to tip,
he answered a question we hadn't asked,

and said: "No, Blake wasn't mad,
Blake wasn't mad at all . . ."

in a way that indicated he was—which
is why we all wanted to see a world

in a grain of sand, and why, that summer,
someone was always saying, "Ah Sun-flower!"

Not the Summer of Love

Everyone else was going to San
Francisco, wearing flowers in their hair,

singing, "Come on people now, smile on your
brother," or "Look what's happening out in

the streets . . . Got a revolution," but we
went East, flying student standby, taking

a cab to the Y, eating the cheapest
things on the menu, still thinking we might

apply at the Kelly Girl place, until
one day we went to Harvard Square and met

Steve from Viet Nam and his best friend Dog
from nowhere, with their guitars and tabs of

LSD, which we were afraid to try
(I am telling you this now with a sigh!).

Moon Landing 1969

I woke that morning at a Diggers in Halifax
and stumbled down the stairs to hear a kid

from Brooklyn read a poem about how fucked
it was that America was landing on the moon.

After that, Catherine and I made breakfast
(a pot of oatmeal mixed with peaches)

for the deserters, draft dodgers, and other
refugees from the war—none of us

visible from outer space—and later
we walked to the park with Richard

and someone with a guitar kept playing
Dylan's "Masters of War" over and over.

We missed the TV shots, the crackling voices—
we only knew the moon looked different.

Lottery

I'd picked him out of all the vagabonds
of those days, even though he often made

me suffer and behave outrageously.
If there is really such a thing as a

"bad influence," he was one, and I learned
how to procrastinate, delay, and quit.

He was my whirligig, my broken star,
the compass that never pointed North. Still,

he could blow a chain of perfect smoke rings,
he was the only blue-eyed soul brother

between here and Chicago, the only
Ezekiel to see the wheels within

the wheels. That's why all bets were off that night,
why the gods hung over those crazy dice.

At Bowdoin

For practical purposes, I had to
pretend I did not exist (I did not

exist) although at night a plate of toast
and cup of tea would disappear. I marked

out places on the map where I might live,
sang "to Susan on the west coast waiting"

and "Oh Canada" in a slip-slide of
Joni Mitchell's silky blues. I was not

there, and when spring came ("tin soldiers and
Nixon's coming"), I was not anywhere.

Once, during those days, I walked through Brunswick
in snow much like the snow that fell back home—

whiter even than the snows of childhood
and snowmen who had melted clean away.

May 1970

He was driving my car. That's one thing
that was wrong, and I didn't know his real

name, but that was an entirely different problem.
If you would have asked me then, I would have

said something analogous to "Freedom's just
another word for nothin' left to lose."

Apparently, I was immune to the usual
entanglements: marriage, a job, some kind of

future. One little white pill was the ticket.
If we had consulted the gurus or even

the local priest, they would have gone pale;
they would have crossed themselves in dismay,

but we went on, with him at the wheel
and that new name tucked between us.

Moving to the Mountains

That spring, Richard Nixon was the president,
and his tin soldiers shot four students

in Ohio. We drove the Dakotas
into Montana, into high places

where the snow was falling, then dropped into
Yellowstone about the twelfth of June.

Waterfalls crashed, and geysers erupted.
Hot springs, the color of morning glories,

bubbled and steamed. We pitched our tent on the
pine needle floor, made a fire in the rain.

In Colorado, our friends were waiting
in a white house in Gilpin County.

All summer we sat on the porch watching
the horses graze, the sky a purple rain.

Yakima

In Yakima, it never stopped raining.
Standing in the unemployment line took

most of the morning. My instinct was to
pretend I knew less than I did, assume

the look everyone wore, admit no dreams.
Against the blur of concrete, the only

brightness was the light in the semaphore.
In Yakima, I heard that he was dead,

but it was later, in Tieton, climbing
up and down the apple trees, that I came

to my conclusion: love was bigger than
mountains, understood every failure;

love never closed the door, never said there
was anything that couldn't be forgiven.

Pentecostals, Washington State, 1970

Our friends warned us before they moved out,
leaving behind a grocery bag full

of pears, of the Pentecostals, who met
in the storefront below the apartment.

The pastor was dark haired and wore a suit,
the first elder looked like Colonel Sanders

and had a wife named Mable Cain—his name
was Bill. We loved those kindhearted people

except that we let them think we were married,
and we felt bad about that lie, even

though we thought we probably would marry
after we had sorted out a few things—

for instance: Where would we live if the Lord
didn't come tomorrow? What would we do?

How We Made It to California

We didn't have anything back then, just
an old Chevrolet and a sackful of

clothes. In the mornings, we toasted our bread
on forks held in front of the space heater.

Each day we went to the orchards where we'd
learned how to fill a bin without breaking

off stems or bruising the apples. We threw
our ladders against the trees like migrants,

and by the end of the season, we had
enough cash to make it down to Berkeley

by way of Cannon Beach and Eureka,
all the way down on Highway 101.

I don't think we were ever happier
than that, living on just about nothing.

Agape House

That's where we lived in California,
somewhere in Oakland, above a liquor store.

We folded copies of a newspaper
called *Right On*, its logo a crucifix

gripped in a Black Power fist, its contents
decidedly Marxist. In the kitchen

I peeled apples and potatoes, while my
boyfriend drank coffee and was forbidden

to sleep with me. Every night we went
to a different Bible study, led

by people who would turn out to be the
leaders of the Children of God. I guess

you could say we felt the spirit leave the
building, that we saw the wolves stealing in.

The Visit

This is the one I like best: Abraham
and the three angels, painted sometime in

the nineteen sixties. I like seeing wings
at rest on the bench where they are sitting,

and Abraham, looking hapless and lost,
while his three visitors visit among

themselves, also their mottled wings and how
their feet dangle down as if for landing.

One is dressed in white, one purple, one blue.
They use their hands to talk; they are talking

so intently they appear not to see
Abraham looking off at something far

away, as if he already knew what
would be required and how it all would end.

At the Rim

We did not take 101 South from San
Francisco; we did not take Highway 1

through Monterey, Pacific Grove, Carmel
and Big Sur. Instead, we went through Fresno

and into Arizona through Needles,
up and around to the Grand Canyon's rim,

where we were the only human beings
for miles and miles, across and up and down.

I stood at the lookout, dizzied by the
colors, the vast canyon, deep as any

mountain is high. He stepped over the
railing, spread his arms as if they were wings,

but he didn't fly away; he just stood
there on one leg, the way birds often do.

Soul Clap Hands

Two things she loved—one for the way
it returned, and the other for the way

it opened—knowing neither one
would make it easier to relinquish

the idea of love. When she looked to
the west, she could see herself as a small

wing on the horizon, a fire burning
for a moment when the sun sank into

the horizon, and she was there in the
flock of birds that twirled like a black cape

over the meadow, and that was also her—
the sudden return, the last note in the box.

The body was only a tattered thing
unless soul clap hands (and yes) sing.

This

Marriage

What we know now that we didn't know then
would fill a small library. We could write

volumes on the subject: how to enter
into it blindly, how to pretend it

never happened; how to make each other
over into something human again.

If only we had relied on something
else or if nothing had really mattered

as we said it did. Even now it's hard
to believe how long we walked on air (or

was it water? We never could agree).
My worst mistake was thinking I could change,

and yours was thinking I never would.

As It Turned Out

We'd been reading the maps all wrong.
We hadn't planned on so much snow,

and the towns we passed
had names we'd never heard of,

and, as it turned out, we'd been
listening to the wrong radio station,

and drove straight into the storm
without hearing the reports that

would have turned us around
had we not been at the very edge

of a chasm, on a ledge that was
beginning to crack and crumble

in the place where we'd just been
standing . . .

What He Could Do

What he could do was the unexpected,
the thing you couldn't ask anyone else

to do, something that lasted all night, some
thing that only made sense to you and to him

because you'd worked out the details and he'd
agreed, and once he's there, he's on your side

and wouldn't complain, no matter how long
the thing drags on, no matter how absurd

the situation, he'd be there waiting
for you, maybe taking a little nap

between the scenes. What he could do was what
you were never sure anyone should do.

What he could do was believe you when you
agreed to say what he wanted to hear.

In New Jersey

We lived in the endless towns, where one street
ran into another—dismal places

between the freeways and darkened train yards.
The red eye of the drug company blinked,

and on the corner someone was always
waiting for the 32. Nights, I worked

in the donut shop. I don't know if we
were married then; I don't think so, but soon

I stopped working there and took the train
up to Chatham to type in amps and volts.

I liked that town and its red brick ways; liked
the post office and its minor miracles.

I didn't mind sitting at the Vari-Typer
for hours, waiting for some small happiness.

The Summer We Delivered Flowers

It was all so petrochemical, so
bio-undegradable, with towns that

never ended before the next one started,
and from the parkway I could see

the houses, one roof after another
and then the smoking oil refineries

and empty lots with piles of tires
and broken glass, from Bayonne to Jersey

City, Elizabeth all the way to Newark—
one town quickly blurring into the next.

Cars were expensive, gas station lines
went all around the block. Nobody was

hiring. All we could do was deliver
flowers for somebody else's wedding.

Moses

Most of the time we went down the Jersey
Shore to Asbury Park by Ocean Grove,

which my sister-in-law called Ocean GRAVE,
or further down to Seaside Heights, across

the bridge from Tom's River, but once we
went over to Long Island, through Newark,

Elizabeth, and Bayonne, up along
the Big L.I.E. to Jones Beach and the Moses

bridges and the Moses water tower
and the Moses bath houses, shuffle boards,

and trash bins. After that, it was all sun
and sand and sea shells. My mother-in-law

dozed on the blanket, while my new husband
and I went far as a wave could take us.

The Italian Deli

I was going to have a baby
in New Jersey—two things I never thought

would happen to me, but it was 1973
and the world had been falling apart

for a decade, starting with that day in Dallas.
Afternoons, when I finally stopped

going to Chatham on the train, I liked to walk
down to the Italian deli in East Orange

and order a pound of thin-sliced capicola,
a loaf of olive bread, and two swans

made of crème-puff pastry filled with whipped cream.
I liked to think I was turning into

an Italian Mama, and all I'd have
to do from then on was say *mangia*!

Things I Learned from My Mother-In-Law

Grocery shop every day. Shop
like a Parisian—get your baguette

in the morning, consult with the butcher
in the afternoon, have a glass of

sherry every night. Never take sides.
Simply listen and withhold judgment. Later,

when she loves him again, she won't
have to remember that you told her to

"kick the bum out." When criticized, affect
a weary or confused expression,

as if the matter under fire is only
vaguely familiar. Pretend you were

listening. Pretend that you are listening
now. Open a secret checking account.

The Hired Man

He was a secret, of course, and his job
was to keep me happy. I didn't pay

well, and I never paid on time, but he
must have liked the hours or the location.

I'm not even sure how it all started,
or whether he worked for me or I

for him; the situation seemed to lack
the usual hierarchy—no CEO.

The benefits, it turned out, were mutual,
though neither of us invested wisely,

so that when we decided to retire,
the returns were sad and small, as often

is the case in these matters. No one falls
in love thinking they'll make a fortune.

Kodak Moments

In this one, he stands in a room without
windows—the inner room where we listened

to the blackbird singing, afternoon light
reaching all the way in to cover us

in gold, just as they sang "Here Comes the Sun."
That day was the beginning of a chain

of lead (not gold); things said that afternoon
wound themselves through all the years that followed.

He is wearing a flannel shirt, a brand
I can't remember now—once the only

kind he'd wear, something from a catalogue.
He looks up, not happy to hear the click

of the camera, warning there will be
reprisals—which explains the next shot. (Bang!)

The Bottom Line

I make a map.
This is the edge of the world;

words end here, dreams too.
Then I make a chart.

This line shows the rise of expectations;
this might be called a crash.

I devise a secret code.
Nothing about it is obvious;

even I can't decipher it.
The recipe calls for cellphones,

answering machines, and modems.
Fingers on the keyboard, silence.

When the bill comes it lists
broken hearts, parted lips, hands.

I pay for it all on time.

In Extremity

Often, I was impatient with words.
I didn't think like a bird,

I wasn't listening the way trees do.
I was sad because my body was all I had,

my hands would never change,
and the mirror would always show the same face.

One night the moon came to the window
where the snow was falling (lovely).

I heard something singing
without the words, a tune

that would never end. "Hope," it said
and perched there in my soul,

just waiting for a plank to break
(a dream I have that causes me to wake).

The Wrong Dress

The dress I wanted to wear was the right dress
to wear that night. You didn't agree, so I

went upstairs to change into the wrong dress,
and because of that I felt strange all night,

and I said the wrong thing to a person
I wouldn't have been talking to had I

been feeling more like myself, and I did
not talk to the right person, the one who

would have understood that I was only
wearing the wrong dress and saying the wrong

thing because I didn't know what else to do.
The word I used was the one I wanted.

You didn't like the sound of it, but that just
convinced me that it was the perfect word.

And Then

The Owl

I hear it for a while before I hear it—
that is, before I realize I'm hearing

a bird call from deep in the woods behind
the house across the street. It's an owl—

a barred owl—I guess, making the familiar
"Who cooks for you, who cooks for you all" call.

If I could see her, I'd see her head swivel
a half circle just before she leans in

and pushes out that cry—one more time—I've
just finished reading Brecht's question about

the dark times and the answer: "Yes, there will
be singing. About the dark times." Why do

these somewhat bitter words make me smile?
Why do I lift my head, shake my hair free,

and leap to my feet, clapping my hands together?

Why We're Here

Don't try to answer that directly.
Think of apples, when they ripen, waiting

for a hand to pull down the branch.
Consider mountains, unclimbed and lonely,

and shores where there's never been a footprint
in the sand, seas where no sails have sailed.

Nothing has ever made a word, and
sentences are as impossible as

thunder without lightning, and what if
no one ever sang or pounded a drum?

What if feet never danced to a tune?
Who else but us would try to name the stars?

Imagine, for a moment, what the world
would be without us. No one to forgive.

Say the Word

Choices we have made or refused,
ways we might have taken once,

times we would not wait,
or times we waited much too long.

Roads we could not follow and the
ones we never found—all those

roads that led to nowhere, all those
hopes that led to nothing—

every one of them is something sacred,
something you can call your own.

Everything you lose you'll find again;
if it's worth the trouble, it will be there.

You can begin again; start all over
any time. You just need to say the word.

Forgotten Dreams

They are excellent dancers, specializing
in the tango, and you have watched them for so long
you know all of the steps.

They are like the moon in the early morning—
a thin circle of silver fading into the sky,
pennies dropped into a deep river.

Some of them zip themselves up and swallow the key;
they climb the fire escape and run across the rooftops,
leaping from one building to another.

They are traveling salesmen hauling their leather
cases filled with hairbrushes and cures; their
lemon pie filling is the best on earth.

Freud says that we forget them for good reason; Jung
says there is nothing reasonable that makes
us happy. I say I want to remember them.

More Flowers Then

I want you to know that I was walking
(just walking) around the marsh as usual,

but it was later (later) in the year
and darker too. There were no dogs

this time—not one (no beagles, no poodles)
and it was cool (not cold, but cool) even

though most of the leaves were green—except for
the sumac. The sumac was red. Along

the edge of the marsh the yellow flowers
were everywhere—such a profusion

of yellow! As if to put a face on
something. The big oak tree by the railroad

seemed (in that darker light) to be holding
a small tree in its arms. More flowers then.

Between the Stars

For a long time, we went on living.
We were casual about it—not wanting

to draw attention to our good fortune.
We asked so little of the universe—

only that it leave us alone, that it
pass us over this year and then the next.

After a while, we seemed invincible.

When our bodies began to betray us,

we were as surprised as they were, looking
into mirrors at faces we didn't

recognize. Now the distance between the stars
mattered to us, and now it didn't. Time,

as always, was the villain, with his scythe
and crooked knife. Oh, how we hated him!

That Moment

It didn't last—that moment I wished for.
I was always making the same mistake,

thinking I could slow down time or erase
the changes it made in everything.

Everything changes. I know that now,
and I am something other than I was

a moment ago before I opened
this book and began to write these words.

How unlikely it is that we should meet!
What sly angel, dressed in feathers and bone,

clapped her hands and named the stars? Notice how
the light is never lost, how it lingers

in the darkest hour, how it changes and
reflects and makes of time a little stay.

Not in the Obituary

There's nothing about how long she could stay
underwater or how many library cards

she had. Nothing about how well
she could keep a secret or how closely

she listened, how she never took sides
in an argument, and there's no mention

of how many sonnets she knew by heart.
The obit doesn't say she hitchhiked

up the coast to Nova Scotia, and there's
nothing about the years in New Jersey,

London? Yes, but how could anyone leave
out London? She made two major mistakes,

but neither one of them was mentioned—
pity! (They had such wondrous results.)

Losing Faith

Thinking about something does not make it
happen. I was thinking about calling

you but I didn't; I was hoping that you
would call me, but the phone never rang. Once

I had the power to will things into
being. I would dream about you and you

would appear from thousands of miles away;
we answered each other before we called.

No one would believe how we were back then.
What I liked the most was the way the old

people smiled at us even though they knew
our fortune was not to be together.

They liked the way we accepted our fate;
they knew that sometimes heaven comes too late.

Summer Days

Shall I compare them? To what? As I
remember, the winds were rough in May,

the lilacs rusted, the peonies scattered,
and now the William Baffin roses

are already losing their first bloom.
Sometimes the warmth we so desired

in January is too hot in July—it's
just the way it goes. The sun beats down

and covers everything in gold; the green
world, which seemed as if it would last forever,

is hazing over the woods and meadows
where a single sumac leaf, burning

like a blaze of fire, hangs at the top
of a bush. Look! you can see it turning.

Pearl

Now, because I chose that turn,
There is no turning, and tomorrow

will never be what could have been
today. I wish I could work the clock,

slowing every minute from then to
now. I wish there was here and here

was where you are. I am coming
to these thoughts gradually, the way

a photograph darkens with
captured light, the way a bird

pecks through the chalky shell,
something building up around

the grain: luminescent, milky,
until at last: the pearl of love.

Living Proof

The fact that I was there,
that you could touch me,

the fact that you could hear
what I said, that we could

walk across the lawns or stand
in the heat together, wilting.

It was better than virtual
reality, better than texting,

better than talking cell to
cell; it was the real thing.

Not that I didn't believe
before, not that proof

was required, but oh! how
seeing helped my unbelief.

Floater

The tiny black sun in my eye
sometimes floats, rimmed in gold,

from the top of the blue sky down
to the green marsh and the willow.

Some days I fold my wings
and fall through the air.

After all these years, I still
don't know what happiness is.

I think it might be this moment
alone with the wind and a song

coming from the radio
inside of the house.

I think it might be this exact
moment. Now. This.

The Red Kayak

Floats in the middle of the green
lawn, under the old willows

away from the lily beds
and the lilac bushes—out where

the shade is deep and the grass
is long. At the edge

of the koi pond, a boy
stands on one leg, watching

for his favorite fish to swim up
from the terrible deep

under the surface. Though he
does not recognize them by name,

all the birds of his childhood are
gathered around him. The sun

dips like a paddle going
into the water.

What To Do

Wake up early, before the lights come on
in the houses on a street that was once

a farmer's field at the edge of a marsh.
Wander from room to room, hoping to find

words that would be enough to keep the soul
alive, words that might be useful or kind

in a world that is more wasteful and cruel
every day. Remind us that we are

like grass that fades, fleeting clouds in the sky,
and then give us just one of those moments

when we were paying attention, when we gave
up everything to see the world in

a grain of sand or to remember
a rainbow in the sky, the heart

leaping up.

That

Open to the South

So I approached my subject from the side,
an angle, not of reposing like Wallace

Steven's great nude—but of agitation:
a figure walking back and forth beneath

a window, a shadow's shadow grasping
at straw. I am not the woman that I

was, though certainly I am all of what
I once was (late and soon) in this too much

with us world wherein we have our being
and breathe: one breath after another, and

then no more. Notice how the oldest words
gather here at the very end, as if

saying what I'd said was enough, as if
I'd planned to strike a match (like Yeats!) and blow.

The Poets

What can I say about my friends,
the poets? That they came later,

after the potters and the painters,
and that they were my family

within the tribe. Finally,
I was at home in the universe.

I can say that the poets lived
in words the way birds live

in trees. Each had a voice
that was unmistakable, and they

never failed to surprise me.
They were quick as foxes,

and they made nothing
happen. They compared

the world to a grain of sand;
they danced and were foolish,

and they learned by going
where they had to go.

The Wordsworth Effect

Is when you return to a place
and it's not nearly as amazing
as you once thought it was,

or when you remember how you felt
about something (or someone) but you know
you'll never feel that way again.

It's when you notice someone has turned
down the volume, and you realize
it was you; when you have the

suspicion that you've met the enemy
and you are it, or when you get
your best ideas from your sister's journal.

Is also—to be fair—the thing that enables
you to walk for miles and miles chanting to
yourself in iambic pentameter

and to travel through Europe with
only a clean shirt, a change of
underwear, a notebook and a pen.

And yes: is when you stretch out
on your couch and summon up ten thousand
daffodils, all dancing in the breeze.

Intimations of Mortality

Dove Cottage is smoke
under a slice of silver moon,
and Dorothy is sitting at the fire,
writing to give "Dear William" pleasure.

She's noted the flowers and their
given names: ranunculus
and crowfoot, primrose,
hackberry and violet.

Coming home, she regretted to see
how the fine new houses
had spoiled the view; then she met
a village woman begging.

Hard times these, she wrote
and ended the night considering
the price of a grave—how much
it cost each time the ground was opened.

Berryman's Hands

Watching him on YouTube as he recites
self-consciously, overdoing it,
"Life, friends, is boring," and then comments
on *Anna Karenina* and how he made
Henry, part tragedy, part disaster, with
some humor, but highly exaggerated,
I notice his white and slender hands, how
tapered and long his fingers are
as he smooths his mustache and rubs
his beard, saying words as if by heart,
stealing a quick glance at the page
from behind his horned-rimmed glasses.

Once I saw him leaving Walter Library,
cutting across the mall on his way to
give a lecture in Ford Hall. I should have
dropped everything and followed him
to hear about Stephen Crane, "that great
poet," or Mistress Bradstreet or the Bard,
but he was talking wildly to himself,
pausing as if he heard another voice,
which he did (and I, that day, did not).

Nemerov

There is so much I never knew—forget
the things I forgot—they're nothing compared
to the depths of my ignorance. Tonight,

for example, I looked up the poet,
Howard Nemerov. I never knew that
Diane Arbus was his sister, or that

he was poet laureate two times. I did
know he liked to drink—two men I know both
told me so, with separate stories based

on things that happened when they met him.
I always remember that sort of thing
(and the smell of whiskey in the Chapel),

but now I'll always put the Nemerovs
together—Howard and Diane. Diane.

After Reading a Postcard from Wallace Stevens

We got your card on Monday. It arrived
with the first frost; the air sharpened by the

thought of the grapes you mention—I *love*
"grapes," and "foxes"—put me in mind of, well,

you-know-what I'm sure.
                              It was hard to see
the mansion house clearly, but the children,

standing at the gate under the spring clouds
looked happy and seemed not to hear despair

beyond the windy sky. They held your bones
gently before they let them fall along the path.

I know that you wish we'd have been there; we
wished that too until we heard the news. Now

we will miss you even more than we did
before. Thanks for the card. It's on the fridge.

Setting Type with Walt Whitman

All of the I's get used up right away.
Next thing,
he cuts himself up into little pieces
like stars
and distributes them
across the universe of the page.

It means letter by letter,
space by space,
the ink
spread carefully, lovingly, across
a dozen rollers,
multitudes
impressed with his barbaric yawp.

It means
this book in your hand,
his voice in your ear, the sparkle
surrounding
the edge of the type, his eye
always regarding
you.

Late March from the Palmer House

for Tim

It's good to think of John Keats
on a rainy day in Chicago
and to read his letter to his friend
Reynolds, the insurance clerk.

We haven't changed much
in two hundred years—Keats sounds
like you, complaining about "poetry
that has a palpable design upon us,"

and I say that your notes
and the attachment (something you
wrote that morning at Vera's) give
me "more pleasure than will the

4th Book of Childe Harold & the whole
of anybody's life & opinions."

On the Spanish Steps, Rome

It wasn't at all like his house
in Hampstead, with its pear tree

and the chairs pushed into place
for the portrait. Outside the window

people gathered on the steps—
an entire soccer team, two monks,

and Elizabeth Bishop's carnival dog.
I felt so melancholy, looking out

at the sweet Italian sky, thinking
of young John Keats and his

"posthumous existence," that
I had to go and sit by his grave

where his name was surely
engraved in stone.

Forgive Me, John Keats

The day we read your "Ode on a Grecian Urn"
I wasn't able to make them see it.

I couldn't get them to hear your voice, to
imagine you standing in a bare room

slowly circling the urn, noticing
the lovers and the piper and the town,

and how it occurred to you that not one
detail would change; no one would ever grow

old there, the leaves would never fall. I tried
to get them to think about Art and Life—

how one is long and the other is short,
how death may be the mother of beauty.

but forgive me, John Keats, I failed to let
them see your hand (still warm) held out to us.

Reading Stanley Plumly

for Stanley Plumly (1939 – 2019)

I'm sitting in a sunlit room, reading
Stanley Plumly. The phone rings—
Tim is in Red Wing, doing something at
the Court House, buying Haralson
apples at the grocery store. I say
stop by on your way back home,
which is what he was hoping to do—
though it would have been ok,
either way (I know that too), so I
go out and walk in the leaves
around the Tower, around the house,
and I see Robert and Art standing
there, so I go over and talk to them
until Tim arrives, which doesn't take
long, and he joins us for a while,
talking about the bookfair on Saturday
and certain poems about autumn
that we all love. Then Art has to go,
and Robert tells a story before he
leaves, and then Tim and I sit on
the front steps in the sun, eating
Haralson apples, and then Tim leaves
and I'm back in the sunlit room
reading Stanley Plumly's poems.

How He Sang

for W. S. Merwin (1927 – 2019)

One of us is gone, one
who learned his song
from the phoenix and
the emperor's golden bird,
who knew the sound of
silence, how it flowed back
and covered everything.

He is gone, who could speak
for the animals and things
that had no names or names
so familiar they were only
shadows of shadows.

His wisdom was in asking
what it is we want to know
what it might be called and
where it might be found.

He had a way of making light
as the darkness was coming on,
of turning sorrow into a song.

Solstice

for Louis Jenkins

The earth is tilted
as far away from
the sun as it can go.
The longest nights
pass like tall ships
on an endless ocean.
We hear nothing, and
then we hear that you
have stopped eating,
that you are fading.
Oh fierce and beautiful
friend! The sun hangs
low on the horizon,
the shadows are long.
I think of how the light
always returns, how
this time you will be
on the other side of it
with the sun and
the moon and stars.

Remembering the Poem

You say the words over and over again
until you know them by heart. Months pass, years,

the poem is like a ghost ship in the desert,
swept over by sand, the outline barely

visible, or it is a faded page
that you will have to reconstruct line by

line from words that stand out of the white blur
like landmarks in a fog. You begin

to recognize it at last—after you
have been walking side by side with it

for a long time, thinking that its face seemed
strange but familiar, and that voice! Where

had you heard that voice? That's when it
starts to come back—all the words again.

And At Last

What I Did Not Know

What I did not know I did not have is
what I was looking for even when I

did not know what it was I did not have.
What I did not have, I would never have

known if I had not had a heart that had
to have it, and, having it, my heart knew

what it hadn't had before and had no
heart to go back to what it once had had.

What heart I had I did not know, but now
what I did not have was not what I did

not know. No, no. Now what I did not know
was what my heart would do now that it had

what it did not know it was looking for—
now that it knew what it was it did not know.

Imagining Happiness

Nothing happened, except that after you'd
gone, I saw your clothes still in the closet,

and the chambray shirt you wore the night
we made dinner for our children (yours, mine)

was draped over the chair in the bedroom.
I noticed your new Eccos on the stairs.

The lawn was going to look good for
at least a week, and then (eventually)

I would go out and imagine myself as you,
trimming away the grass in long green strips.

In the garage, I remembered that kiss
just before you left, and how the tree saw

and the new lawn cart looked more promising
than yesterday's rainbow after the storm.

Your Shirt

I know I said you have too many shirts;
I implied that you are vain (I know!),

but the shirt hanging over the kitchen chair
(with the cuffs folded back and the collar

rolled out—the one you bought just yesterday,
with the pastel colors and a pattern

you said was like tattersall except much
lighter weight than all the others—which

is why you had to have it)—that shirt,
the one you almost didn't buy because

of me—that shirt is a reminder of
the way you put your arms around me

when I am cold and lost, how you always
have more to give than I thought I needed.

The Way You Do What You Do

I love the way you care about your clothes—
that shirt, for example, from L.L. Bean,

the one my mother said she liked (your
new favorite) and the way you pick out

your jacket or shoes, and the way you make
dinner, surrounded by garlic paper and

onion skins, carrot peelings, half-used
cans of tomato paste, pools of olive oil,

pots of boiling pasta and red sauces
on the stove and you, chopping and timing,

and, of course, the way you think about the
wines in our cellar and what would be

right with dinner, and afterwards (the way
you always think about what comes after).

Zippers

Something about
the way one side
needs to fit into
the other—end to end
and teeth lined up
just right—
happens
only when I feel good
about the chance
that anything
will ever line up right.

What I mean is this:
The other day
in Eddie Bauer, trying
on coats from the clearance rack,
I found
each zipper
a challenge,
and after a while
you couldn't stand
to watch me fail
and fail
again,
and so you pulled
me close
the way one does
a child,
and for a moment
everything
came together.

Now (and Hereafter)

If there is nothing here under the bone
where the heart is resting, nothing risked

in the saying, nothing to lose in the way
you touch me (so carefully), then (darling)

where would be the wonder in the wishing
when the stone is tossed into the river,

when the coin is spinning in the air,
when the feather drifts up on the wind?

Where—if there is nothing out there—are we
then when we lift our glasses full of wine

and say: To us, to life, to the future,
to what may come (now and hereafter).

At the Greek Restaurant

They were understaffed, and the staff they had
just took their time—as if people weren't

glaring at them from the tables they'd been
sitting at for ten god-awful minutes—

"I mean, can you believe it? Stuck there for
ten entire minutes, with no bread and no

water—not even a menu!" None of
that mattered to us; we'd just had some bad

news and couldn't bear the ordinary
rituals of evening this once. You said

we should go to Greece, and for a moment
I could see a flash of Aegean blue above

the white walls of Santorini, but then
the waiter came, and we ordered salad.

If Only This Moment Always

Midsummer, nothing between
green and the greenest green.

A lawn mower stops somewhere
beyond, and we can hear the birds

again. The wind. Everything
lifts and moves at once; the rains

that fell last night sink deeper
into the shadows on the lawn.

Doors slam in the distance,
wind chimes ring and rattle,

then the phone, and there you are,
calling from the mountains,

across the long flat lands,
happier, you say, than ever.

From Here

According to the GPS, we are
where we should be, on just the right highway

going West for the next twelve hundred miles,
stopping twice for gas and another for

coffee and glazed donuts. It always works,
even when you decide (for one reason

or another) that the little arrow
moving forward on the screen cannot

possibly be us and that we are now
hopelessly lost somewhere in Nebraska

between Omaha's forever neon motels
and the muddy feedlots of Milford.

It's good to know that according to the G-
PS, we are exactly where we should be.

The Summer We Stayed Home

That was the summer we stayed home—
no trans-Atlantic flights, no cross-country

road trips—not even a weekend
on the North Shore. You planted roses

and went back and forth to the
garden store like a Ping-Pong ball—

I baked cakes and looked at all
the houses you found on Zillow.

Sometimes I worked on a poem.
What did we learn from staying home?

It's true: our bed is comfortable,
and we are surrounded by books,

the view of the marsh is lovely,
it's only a few miles to the Arboretum,

and the big lake is just beyond that.
At home, we didn't have to eat out every

night—though we remembered
(fondly) the Bosnian restaurant in

Dubrovnik and that Indian place
in London. London. How we missed London.

Beautiful Yesterday

You arrived, wearing the time
like another skin,
a container that contained
everything we desire
of a summer's day: heat
sinking into our backs and shoulders,
the wind lifting hair
slightly, setting off highlights, brushing
along a cheekbone and catching—there at
the throat.

How good it is to have a body,
to sit in the garden reading poetry
and talking across the miles,
saying what we can only say
today, this yesterday's day
all of our tomorrows become.

Now that our days are numbered,
why not make each of them
as beautiful as the one we lived
in today, admiring flowers
that opened (full throated to
greet us) and now lie
blasted and scattered
on the ground
while the exquisite buds
of morning have opened in profusion.

Blessing the World

I mean the one that surrounds us,
the one that causes such suffering
and refuses to let us go. I mean
that one,

and the one full of stupidity—the one
that some of us scroll endlessly
doom-raged and cursing—that one
especially.

I mean what world
we have left
once we have covered the meadows
with condos and strip malls;

I mean the poor ruined earth
beneath our deals, our markets and shares—
where everything has a price
even here, even now—which is why

we must bless the world
with the part of us that made
the music and the paintings,
the bridges and airplanes; the dictionaries

where the word for what we will do
has not yet been invented.

Maybe Arizona

When I hear you humming
in the room below this one,
I know the world will
never be as lonely as it once was,

and when I see the birds
coming to the feeders,
now filled with seeds you bought
at The Wild Bird Store,

I assume we will
be here forever
feeding the birds.

So when you say
you'd like to go someplace
warm and sunny,
I think:

Where will the birds go?
Whose eye will be on the sparrow?

On the Island

I stood in the doorway, listening,
as on an island in an old country—

all chalk and blue sky. What I wanted
was a metaphor for what we are now,

as like to us as is the wind to wing,
mine to mind, love always wanting to live

on the rim of a rhyme, making of what I
could not hear (that herd of reindeer moving

silently and very fast across the tip
of the planet) a heart that would sustain

me on the island—I, being simply a name
(and what's in that but a string of letters?).

There. You see? I've built us a little nest—
here we will remain, and silence be the rest.